am Spirit

THE HOUSTON TEXANS

BY

MARK STEWART

Content Consultant
Jason Aikens

NORWOOD HOUSE PRESS

CHICAGO, ILLINOIS

Norwood House Press
P.O. Box 316598
Chicago, Illinois 60631

For information regarding Norwood House Press, please visit our website at:
www.norwoodhousepress.com or call 866-565-2900.

PHOTO CREDITS:
All photos courtesy of Getty Images except the following:
Topps, Inc. (7, 9, 21 bottom, 22 top, 29, 34 left, 35 top left & bottom right,
36, 37, 39, 43); Black Book Partners Archives (20), Matt Richman (48 top).
Cover photo: Doug Benc/Getty Images
Special thanks to Topps, Inc.

Editor: Mike Kennedy
Designer: Ron Jaffe
Project Management: Black Book Partners, LLC.
Research: Evan Frankel
Special thanks to: Jennifer Schmiedekamp

LIBRARY OF CONGRESS CATALOGING-IN-PUBLICATION DATA

Stewart, Mark, 1960-
   The Houston Texans / by Mark Stewart ; content consultant, Jason Aikens.
      p. cm. -- (Team spirit)
   Includes bibliographical references and index.
   Summary: "Presents the history, accomplishments and key personalities of
the Houston Texans football team. Includes timelines, quotes, maps, glossary
and websites"--Provided by publisher.
   ISBN-13: 978-1-59953-207-3 (library edition : alk. paper)
   ISBN-10: 1-59953-207-7 (library edition : alk. paper) 1. Houston Texans
(Football team)--History--Juvenile works. 2. Football--History. I. Aikens,
Jason. II. Title.
   GV956.H69S84 2008
   796.332'64097641411--dc22
                                                              2008012899

COVER PHOTO: The Texans celebrate a touchdown during a 2007 game.

Table of Contents

CHAPTER	PAGE
Meet the Texans	4
Way Back When	6
The Team Today	10
Home Turf	12
Dressed for Success	14
We Won!	16
Go-To Guys	20
On the Sidelines	24
One Great Day	26
Legend Has It	28
It Really Happened	30
Team Spirit	32
Timeline	34
Fun Facts	36
Talking Football	38
For the Record	40
Pinpoints	42
Play Ball	44
Glossary	46
Places to Go	47
Index	48

SPORTS WORDS & VOCABULARY WORDS: In this book, you will find many words that are new to you. You may also see familiar words used in new ways. The glossary on page 46 gives the meanings of football words, as well as "everyday" words that have special football meanings. These words appear in **bold type** throughout the book. The glossary on page 47 gives the meanings of vocabulary words that are not related to football. They appear in ***bold italic type*** throughout the book.

Meet the Texans

A football team and its fans usually grow up together, kind of like a big family. The Houston Texans are different. They are a new team with "old" fans. The Texans began playing in 2002, but their hometown fans have a history with **professional** football that stretches back to 1960.

Houston is known for giving young players a chance to shine in the **National Football League (NFL)**. In their short history, the Texans have enjoyed amazing victories and suffered heartbreaking defeats. Along the way, they have learned what it takes to reach the next level.

This book tells the story of the Texans. They have built their team slowly and carefully. They have gone through the ups and downs that every **expansion team** experiences. Their fans have already "seen it all" and are willing to wait for a winner to *emerge*. It is the beginning of a whole new football *tradition* in one of the NFL's great football towns.

Matt Schaub congratulates Andre Johnson after a touchdown during a 2007 game.

Way Back When

From 1960 to 1995, pro football was the most popular sport in Houston, Texas. The city's first team was the Oilers. They played in the **American Football League (AFL)** for 10 seasons before joining the NFL in 1970. Houston loved its Oilers.

That is why the city's fans were shocked and disappointed when the Oilers moved to Tennessee in 1997. A year later, a group of

investors led by Bob McNair asked the NFL to consider Houston for a new team. The league was set to expand. The NFL promised Houston fans that they would have their new team when the league expanded in 2002.

There was much work to do. The team needed a new stadium, a new uniform, and a new name. Construction soon started on the NFL's first *retractable*-roof stadium. Artists began designing team colors and a *logo*. And the team picked its name from five options—Apollos, Bobcats,

LEFT: Bob McNair announces a pick during the expansion draft.
RIGHT: Jamie Sharper, one of Houston's first defensive stars.

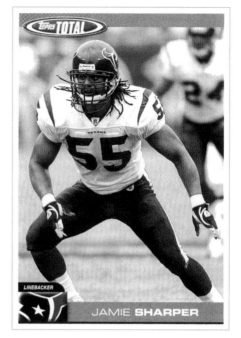

Stallions, Texans, and Wildcatters. With help from 65,000 fans who voted online, Texans was the final choice. The team also hired its first head coach, Dom Capers.

The Texans would be part of the new **South Division** of the **American Football Conference (AFC)**. They were matched with three good teams, the Indianapolis Colts, Jacksonville Jaguars, and Tennessee Titans. Houston fans looked forward to a great *rivalry* with the Titans, the team that had once been the Oilers. They were also excited for the team's first regular-season game against Texas's other team, the Dallas Cowboys.

The Texans were allowed to select players from other teams in a special **expansion draft**. Their first pick was Tony Boselli, an **All-Pro blocker** from the Jaguars. They also took defensive stars Aaron Glenn and Gary Walker. Jamie Sharper, a linebacker who had helped the Baltimore Ravens win the **Super Bowl**, also signed with the Texans. Unfortunately, Boselli was injured and did not play for Houston. The Texans relied on their defensive stars to lead the team.

On offense, the Texans looked to quarterback David Carr. He was the team's first choice in the 2002 NFL draft. The Texans hoped their defense would be strong enough to allow their young passer to learn and grow. Houston won four games in its first season. One of those victories was over the Cowboys in the team's first game.

In 2003, two **rookies** energized the Texans. Receiver Andre Johnson gave Carr a great target, and Domanick Williams sparked Houston's running game. In their second season, the Texans improved with five victories and played well in losses to some very good teams. In 2004, the team went 7–9.

Many fans believed the Texans could make the **playoffs** in 2005, but Houston took a step backwards. The team won only two games and finished with the worst record in the NFL. The fans had been patient. Now they wanted a winner. The Texans brought in a new coach and began to rebuild the team for the future.

LEFT: Andre Johnson, who joined the Texans in 2003 and quickly became the team's top receiver.   **ABOVE**: David Carr, the quarterback who led Houston in its early years.

The Team Today

New players and a new attitude made the Texans one of the toughest teams in the AFC in 2006 and 2007. They began to win the close games they had once let slip away. The Texans also showed they could make winning plays at key moments. Defensive stars DeMeco Ryans, Mario Williams, Dunta Robinson, and Amobi Okoye led a total team effort.

With a solid defense to build on, new coach Gary Kubiak had the job of creating a more powerful offense. He began looking for strong running backs, receivers, blockers, and a new quarterback. This was a difficult task. The Texans traded for **veterans**, signed **free agents**, and **drafted** young stars.

There are no easy opponents in Houston's division. The team faces a different challenge every week. The fans are rooting for the Texans to reach the Super Bowl, but they are smart enough to know that champions are built one step at a time. Over the next few years, Houston's story should be one of the best in football.

Mario Williams and Amobi Okoye, two of the young stars who helped make Houston's defense one of the best in the NFL.

Home Turf

The Texans play in a stadium that was built near the Astrodome, Houston's famous domed baseball stadium. When the Astrodome opened in 1965, fans called it the "Eighth Wonder of the World." The Texans' stadium is impressive, too. It is part of a large sports and convention complex. Houston's stadium is also used to host rodeos.

The Texans' stadium was built with a retractable roof. No other NFL stadium had this kind of roof, which rolls back in two five-piece sections from above the 50-yard line. The roof can open and close in as little as seven minutes. The Texans play on a grass field, which needs sunlight to stay in good shape. For this reason, the roof on the stadium is often left open.

BY THE NUMBERS

- *There are 71,500 seats for football in the Texans' stadium.*
- *The Texans beat the Dallas Cowboys 19–10 in the stadium's first game.*
- *Super Bowl XXXVIII was played in the Texans' stadium in February 2004. The New England Patriots defeated the Carolina Panthers 32–29.*

Even with the roof closed, there is plenty of light in the Texans' stadium. It was named Reliant Stadium during the team's first season.

Dressed for Success

Houston's team colors are red, white, and blue. The Texans use special versions of these colors known as Deep Steel Blue, Battle Red, and Liberty White. The team chose them as a salute to its home state.

The Texans wear a blue helmet with a bull's head on the side. The bull is drawn to **resemble** the flag of Texas, including the state's five-pointed star. The points stand for pride, courage, strength, tradition, and independence. Houston also uses a logo with the letters *HT*.

The Texans wear blue jerseys or white jerseys for most of their games. Sometimes, they feature red jerseys. These games are known as Bull Red Day. The fans dress in red to match the players. In 2007, the Texans wore red jerseys and red pants for the first time, which proved to be a popular combination.

Aaron Glenn models the uniform from the team's first season.

UNIFORM BASICS

The football uniform has three important parts—
- Helmet
- Jersey
- Pants

Helmets used to be made out of leather, and they did not have facemasks—ouch! Today, helmets are made of super-strong plastic. The uniform top, or jersey, is made of thick fabric. It fits snugly around a player so that tacklers cannot grab it and pull him down. The pants come down just over the knees.

There is a lot more to a football uniform than what you see on the outside. Air can be pumped inside the helmet to give it a snug, padded fit. The jersey covers shoulder pads, and sometimes a rib protector called a flak jacket. The pants include pads that protect the hips, thighs, *tailbone*, and knees.

Football teams have two sets of uniforms—one dark and one light. This makes it easier to tell two teams apart on the field. Almost all teams wear their dark uniforms at home and their light ones on the road.

DeMeco Ryans wears the all-red uniform that Houston introduced in 2007.

We Won!

The eyes of Texas were upon the city of Houston at the start of the 2002 NFL season. The league scheduled a showdown between the Lone Star State's two teams. In their first regular-season game ever, the Texans hosted the Dallas Cowboys.

The game was played on a Sunday night, long after the NFL's other opening-day contests had ended. Millions of football fans tuned in to see the Battle of Texas. NFL Commissioner Paul Tagliabue attended the game to help welcome the Texans to the league.

The fans at Reliant Stadium were buzzing with excitement. The Texans were a brand-new team. No one expected them to win many games. For Houston fans, the contest against the Cowboys was their Super Bowl. The Minnesota Vikings were the last expansion team to win its opening game. That had happened more than four *decades* earlier.

The first time the Texans had the ball, they shocked the Cowboys with a long pass on their first play. Dallas was flagged for a 43-yard penalty. Three plays later, David Carr fired a 19-yard touchdown pass to tight end Billy Miller. The stadium erupted in cheers. The Texans were actually ahead!

LEFT: David Carr throws a pass in Houston's first game.
RIGHT: The Texans hug Billy Miller after his touchdown catch.

In the second quarter, Aaron Glenn **intercepted** a pass by the Cowboys. Moments later, Kris Brown kicked a field goal to make the score 10–0. Dallas fought back to tie the game, but the Texans did not panic. Early in the fourth quarter, Carr threw a 69-yard bomb to Corey Bradford to give Houston a 17–10 lead. Near the end of the game, Seth Payne tackled Dallas quarterback Quincy Carter in his own end zone for a safety, which was good for two more points.

With two minutes left, everyone in the stadium was standing and cheering. As soon as the last play was over, the fans streamed onto the field to celebrate. In their first game, against their biggest rival, the Texans pulled out an amazing 19–10 victory.

ABOVE: The Texans gang up to make a tackle against the Dallas Cowboys.
RIGHT: Aaron Glenn reacts to the cheers after his interception.

Go-To Guys

To be a true star in the NFL, you need more than fast feet and a big body. You have to be a "go-to guy"—someone the coach wants on the field at the end of a big game. Texans fans have had a lot to cheer about over the years, including these great stars ...

THE PLAYERS

DAVID CARR — Quarterback

- BORN: 7/21/1979
- PLAYED FOR TEAM: 2002 TO 2006

In 2002, the Texans made rookie David Carr their starting quarterback and asked him to learn on the job. He was **sacked** 76 times that year, more than any passer in NFL history. In 2006, Carr led the league by completing more than 68 percent of his passes.

LEFT: David Carr
TOP RIGHT: Andre Johnson
BOTTOM RIGHT: Domanick Williams

JAMIE SHARPER   Linebacker

- BORN: 11/23/1974
- PLAYED FOR TEAM: 2002 TO 2004

Jamie Sharper was a tackling machine during his three seasons with Houston. In all, he made more than 400 tackles for the Texans. Sharper had the strength to bring down powerful running backs and the speed to chase after fast receivers.

ANDRE JOHNSON   Receiver

- BORN: 7/1/1981
- FIRST SEASON WITH TEAM: 2003

Andre Johnson was big, strong, and fast. He had a special skill for catching passes while two defenders covered him. Johnson led the NFL with 103 catches in 2006. He caught three passes for 73 yards to help the AFC win the 2007 **Pro Bowl**.

DOMANICK WILLIAMS   Running Back

- BORN: 10/1/1980
- PLAYED FOR TEAM: 2003 TO 2005

Houston fans knew Domanick Williams as Domanick Davis when he joined the team. He changed his last name while playing for the Texans. Williams was the first player in NFL history to be named Rookie of the Week four weeks in a row.

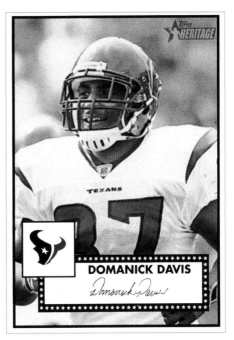

THE PLAYERS

DUNTA ROBINSON   Defensive Back

- BORN: 4/11/1982
- FIRST SEASON WITH TEAM: 2004

In high school, Dunta Robinson was a great **all-around** athlete who played football and basketball and was a sprinter on the track team. The Texans took him with their first pick in the 2004 NFL draft. Robinson quickly became one of the team's defensive leaders. He intercepted six passes as a rookie and sacked All-Pro quarterback Peyton Manning twice.

MARIO WILLIAMS   Defensive Lineman

- BORN: 1/31/1985
- FIRST SEASON WITH TEAM: 2006

The Texans passed on hometown favorite Vince Young to get Mario Williams with the first pick in the 2006 NFL draft. They needed a great pass rusher to compete against teams in the AFC South. As a rookie, Williams learned different *strategies* to *overpower* opposing blockers. A year later, he set a team record with 14 sacks and was voted All-Pro.

TOP LEFT: Dunta Robinson
BOTTOM LEFT: Mario Williams
TOP RIGHT: DeMeco Ryans
BOTTOM RIGHT: Amobi Okoye

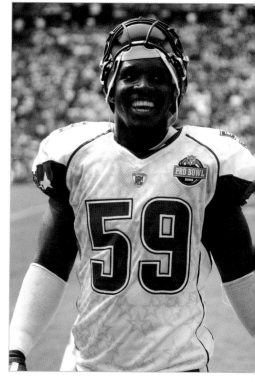

DeMECO RYANS — Linebacker

- Born: 7/28/1984
- First Season with Team: 2006

DeMeco Ryans was a fast and strong linebacker in college. The Texans believed he could be even better in the NFL. Ryans made 12 tackles in his first game with Houston. Before long, he was known as one of the best linebackers in the league. Ryans was named the NFL's Defensive **Rookie of the Year** in 2006. He played in his first Pro Bowl the following season.

AMOBI OKOYE — Defensive Lineman

- Born: 6/10/1987
- First Season with Team: 2007

How young is too young to play in the NFL? Amobi Akoye was just 19 when the Texans drafted him in 2007. This made him the youngest player in the NFL since the 1960s. Okoye played like a veteran who had been in the league for a decade. After his first four games, he was voted Rookie of the Month.

23

On the Sidelines

When the Texans had to choose their first coach, they turned to Dom Capers. He had been the first coach of the Carolina Panthers when they came into the NFL in 1995. Capers proved he knew his stuff when he led the Panthers to the championship game of the **National Football Conference (NFC)** in their second year. He was a master at putting together the right pieces of a good defense.

Capers coached the Texans for four seasons. During that time, Houston played some amazing defensive games. The offense was slow to improve, however. In 2006, Gary Kubiak replaced Capers. Kubiak was known for his talent with quarterbacks. He helped the San Francisco 49ers and Denver Broncos win three Super Bowls. He was also the backup to All-Pro passer John Elway for nine years.

When Kubiak agreed to coach the Texans, he was coming home. As a high school athlete in Houston, he was All-State in football, basketball, baseball, and track. Kubiak once held the Texas high school record for passing yards.

Gary Kubiak discusses a play with Matt Schaub during a 2007 game.

One Great Day

Every game between the Texans and Tennessee Titans is a big game. Houston fans have not forgotten how Tennessee "took" its team away. Also, the Texans and Titans are members of the same division, the AFC South. Every victory and loss is huge.

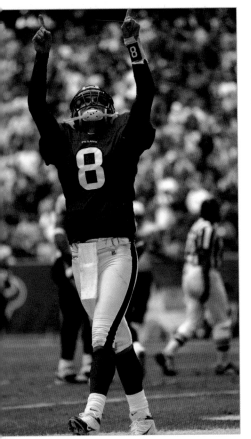

In 2004, the Texans faced the Titans in October. The game was played in Tennessee, and Houston won 20-10. When the Titans traveled to Texas for the rematch, they were looking for payback!

Steve McNair, a hero in his days with the Houston Oilers, put on a show for his old fans. He threw two touchdown passes in the first half for Tennessee, and the Titans ran for another. They led 21–3 at the start of the third quarter.

At that point, David Carr took over. He threw two touchdown passes of his own and guided the Texans to a third score. Houston now led 24–21. McNair and the Titans came

roaring back and moved the ball into Houston territory. They needed a field goal to tie the game and a touchdown to go ahead. The Texans stood tough. Houston's Antwan Peek tackled McNair, and the ball bounced free. Kailee Wong pounced on the **fumble** for the Texans.

Moments later, Andre Davis ran right up the middle for a 41-yard touchdown to make the final score 31–21. The victory was even sweeter because it dropped the Titans into last place in the division behind the Texans.

"It started ugly," Carr said after the game, "but we didn't get *discouraged*, and we just kept plugging away."

LEFT: David Carr celebrates after a touchdown against the Tennessee Titans.
ABOVE: The Texans get tough on defense in their 31–21 victory.

Legend Has It

Who has the "longest" leg in the NFL?

LEGEND HAS IT that Kris Brown does. Other kickers have made longer field goals, but no one has booted more 50-yarders in the same game than Brown. In a 2007 contest against the Miami Dolphins, he kicked five field goals—including successful attempts of 54 yards (twice) and 57 yards. Brown's 57-yarder won the game 22–19 with one second left.

ABOVE: Kris Brown celebrates after his game-winning kick against the Miami Dolphins.   **RIGHT**: A trading card shows Mario Williams ready to make a tackle.

Who is Mario Williams's favorite quarterback to sack?

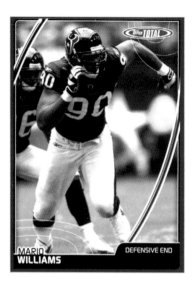

LEGEND HAS IT that Vince Young is. Many Houston fans complained when the Texans skipped over Young in the 2006 draft and took Williams with the first pick instead. Williams never forgot how the fans reacted. Their response made him try extra-hard against the Tennessee Titans, the team that eventually picked Young. When the Texans play the Titans, Young always has an eye on Williams.

Who once threw a football as the first pitch in a baseball game?

LEGEND HAS IT that Bob McNair did. On the day that McNair announced that Houston's new team would be called the Texans, he was invited to throw the traditional "first pitch" at a baseball game between the Houston Astros and Florida Marlins. McNair walked out to the pitcher's mound, but he had a different idea. Instead of throwing a baseball, the Texans' owner tossed a football to home plate. The "catcher" was Astros owner Drayton McLane.

It Really Happened

Sometimes a football team just can't seem to move the ball forward. The Texans had a day like that near the end of their first season. They were playing the Pittsburgh Steelers, who ended up winning 10 games that year. The Steelers had a very good defense. On this day, however, the Houston defense was even better. They had to be—the Texans recorded just one first down on offense in the last 57 minutes of the game!

The Houston defense made its first big play in the first quarter when Pittsburgh's Tommy Maddox fumbled the ball. Kenny Wright of the Texans scooped it up and ran 40 yards for a touchdown. The next time the Steelers had the ball, Aaron Glenn intercepted a pass by Maddox and returned it 70 yards for a touchdown.

The Steelers responded with two field goals to cut the lead to 14–6. Pittsburgh fans got ready to watch their team make a great *comeback*. The Texans, meanwhile, had no luck against the Pittsburgh defense. They gained a total of 47 yards all day.

The Steelers, however, continued to make mistakes. They fumbled a punt, and Kris Brown kicked a field goal to give the Texans a 17–6

James Simmons flashes a big smile after recovering a fumble against the Pittsburgh Steelers.

lead. With two minutes left, Glenn intercepted another pass and raced 65 yards for his second touchdown of the day.

The final score was 24–6. The Houston defense had done a great job when it counted most. Pittsburgh gained 422 yards but could not score a touchdown. Houston coach Dom Capers awarded the game ball to his defense. Texans quarterback David Carr joked afterwards, "They should take the game ball they got and throw it at us!"

Team Spirit

The Texans and their fans take home games very seriously. Their favorite chant is, "We must protect this house!" On those special days when the team wears its all-red uniforms, the fans dress in red, too.

The fans screaming the loudest at Texans games are often seated behind the north end zone. This area is called the Bull Pen. People in these seats especially love Toro, the team's **mascot**. Toro—which is Spanish for "bull"—wears jersey number one and roams the field during games. He shares the sidelines with the Bull Pen Pep Band and the Texans' cheerleaders.

Before kickoff, fans throw big tailgate parties in the parking lot. Many families visit the Fanatic Fan Zone, which is located between the stadium and the Astrodome. After games, fans stay in their seats for the "5th Quarter"—a video review of the game, along with highlights from other NFL games. Later, many fans gather at the team's practice field for a Lone Star Club party.

Houston fans love their team. Here, they celebrate with Andre Johnson after a touchdown on a Bull Red Day.

Timeline

In this timeline, each Super Bowl is listed under the year it was played. Remember that the Super Bowl is held early in the year and is actually part of the previous season. For example, Super Bowl XLII was played on February 3rd, 2008, but it was the championship of the 2007 NFL season.

1999
The NFL announces that Houston will get a new team.

2002
The Texans win their first game, against the Dallas Cowboys.

2003
Aaron Glenn and Gary Walker start in the Pro Bowl.

2004
Super Bowl XXXVIII is played in Reliant Stadium.

Jabar Gaffney, a star on the 2002 team.

Gary Walker

Andre
Johnson

DeMeco Ryans
makes a tackle
during a
2007 game.

2006
Andre Johnson leads the
NFL with 103 catches.

2008
DeMeco Ryans plays
in his first Pro Bowl.

2005
Jerome Mathis is named
All-Pro as a kick returner.

2007
The Texans go 6–2 at home
and finish with eight victories.

Jerome
Mathis

Ron Dayne,
a star for the
2007 team.

Fun Facts

LUCKY SEVEN

In 2003, the Texans had the NFL Rookie of the Week seven times. Domanick Williams won the award five times, and Andre Johnson won it twice.

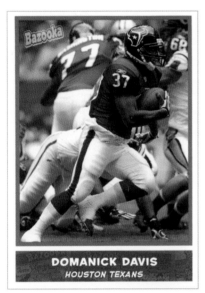

DOMANICK DAVIS
HOUSTON TEXANS

HAPPY RETURN

In 2005, Jerome Mathis set a team record with a 99-yard touchdown on a kickoff return. After the season, he was voted to the Pro Bowl.

NAME THAT TEAM

In 2002, Houston became the fifth pro team to use the name "Texans." In 1952, an NFL team called the Dallas Texans played for one season. From 1960 to 1962, the Kansas City Chiefs played in Dallas and were also called the Texans. In 1974, a team called the Houston Texans joined the **World Football League (WFL)**. Later, in 1995, a team called the San Antonio Texans played in the **Canadian Football League (CFL)**.

ABOVE: A trading card of Domanick Williams, which shows his last name as Davis.
RIGHT: A trading card shows Andre Johnson wearing number 15.

RICE IS NICE

Andre Johnson was given number 15 when he joined the Texans in 2003. Johnson later asked for number 80. It was a **_tribute_** to his hero, superstar Jerry Rice.

ON THE POSITIVE SIDE

In a 2006 game against the Oakland Raiders, the Texans had –5 yards passing, but they still won. Houston's runners gained 129 yards, and the defense forced five **turnovers**.

SMART KID

Amobi Okoye was the youngest player ever taken in the first round of the NFL draft. He was accepted to the University of Louisville at age 15. He graduated when he was 19.

OPEN SEASON

When the Texans beat the Miami Dolphins to start the 2003 season, they became the first NFL expansion team to win their first two season openers.

Talking Football

"I am just a true football player who loves the game, just high-energy, high-passion every time I step on the field, just having fun."
—*DeMeco Ryans, on what motivates him*

"It's one of the toughest positions. It's physically challenging. Sometimes you're out there on an island."
—*Dom Capers, on how hard it is for a college defensive back to adjust to the NFL*

"The people who are coming out today are a lot more athletic, bigger, stronger, faster."
—*Gary Kubiak on the difference between the NFL now and when he played*

ABOVE: Dom Capers   **RIGHT**: Matt Schaub

"It's huge in this league to go on the road and play in a tough environment against good football teams and come away with a victory. That's the test of a true champion and a good football team."
—Matt Schaub, on one of the toughest challenges in the NFL

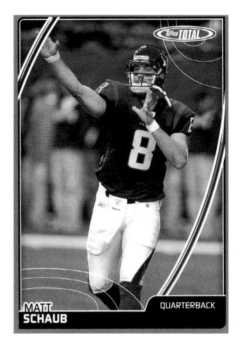

"I'll trade that sack any day for a win."
—Amobi Okoye, on putting the team's goals before his goals

"My biggest goal is just to go out there and make plays, no matter when it is. Even if I don't make a tackle, as long as I know I helped make that play. Just going out there and letting it loose, that's all I'm worried about."
—Mario Williams, on being a team player

"We support each other, we help each other as much as we can. We're definitely one big happy family."
—Joel Dressen, on the secret to Houston's team spirit

For the Record

T he great Texans teams and players have left their marks on the record books. These are the "best of the best" …

TEXANS AWARD WINNERS

WINNER	AWARD	YEAR
Domanick Williams	Offensive Rookie of the Year	2003
DeMeco Ryans	Defensive Rookie of the Year	2006

RIGHT: Domanick Williams looks for an opening in the defense. In 2003, he won the award as the NFL's best rookie on offense.
FAR RIGHT: Mario Williams and DeMeco Ryans are ready for a play to come their way. Ryans was voted the NFL's top defensive rookie in 2006.

Pinpoints

T he history of a football team is made up of many smaller stories. These stories take place all over the map—not just in the city a team calls "home." Match the pushpins on these maps to the Team Facts and you will begin to see the story of the Texans unfold!

TEAM FACTS

1 Houston, Texas—*The team has played here since 2002.*

2 Irving, Texas—*Kris Brown was born here.*

3 Lafayette, Louisiana—*Domanick Williams was born here.*

4 Bessemer, Alabama—*DeMeco Ryans was born here.*

5 Miami, Florida—*Andre Johnson was born here.*

6 Richlands, North Carolina—*Mario Williams was born here.*

7 Richmond, Virginia—*Jamie Sharper was born here.*

8 Athens, Georgia—*Dunta Robinson was born here.*

9 Cambridge, Ohio—*Dom Capers was born here.*

10 Berlin, New Jersey—*Ron Dayne was born here.*

11 Bakersfield, California—*David Carr was born here.*

12 Anambra State, Nigeria—*Amobi Okoye was born here.*

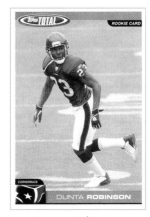

Dunta Robinson

Play Ball

Football is a sport played by two teams on a field that is 100 yards long. The game is divided into four 15-minute quarters. Each team must have 11 players on the field at all times. The group that has the ball is called the offense. The group trying to keep the offense from moving the ball forward is called the defense.

A football game is made up of a series of "plays." Each play starts and ends with a referee's signal. A play begins when the center snaps the ball between his legs to the quarterback. The quarterback then gives the ball to a teammate, throws (or "passes") the ball to a teammate, or runs with the ball himself. The job of the defense is to tackle the player with the ball or stop the quarterback's pass. A play ends when the ball (or player holding the ball) is "down." The offense must move the ball forward at least 10 yards every four downs. If it fails to do so, the other team is given the ball. If the offense has not made 10 yards after three downs—and does not want to risk losing the ball—it can kick (or "punt") the ball to make the other team start from its own end of the field.

At each end of a football field is a goal line, which divides the field from the end zone. A team must run or pass the ball over the goal line to score a touchdown, which counts for six points. After scoring a touchdown, a team can try a short kick for one "extra point," or try again to run or pass across the goal line for two points. Teams can score three points from anywhere on the field by kicking the ball between the goal posts. This is called a field goal.

The defense can score two points if it tackles a player while he is in his own end zone. This is called a safety. The defense can also score points by taking the ball away from the offense and crossing the opposite goal line for a touchdown. The team with the most points after 60 minutes is the winner.

Football may seem like a very hard game to understand, but the more you play and watch football, the more "little things" you are likely to notice. The next time you are at a game, look for these plays:

PLAY LIST

BLITZ—A play where the defense sends extra tacklers after the quarterback. If the quarterback sees a blitz coming, he passes the ball quickly. If he does not, he can end up at the bottom of a very big pile!

DRAW—A play where the offense pretends it will pass the ball, and then gives it to a running back. If the offense can "draw" the defense to the quarterback and his receivers, the running back should have lots of room to run.

FLY PATTERN—A play where a team's fastest receiver is told to "fly" past the defensive backs for a long pass. Many long touchdowns are scored on this play.

SQUIB KICK—A play where the ball is kicked a short distance on purpose. A squib kick is used when the team kicking off does not want the other team's fastest player to catch the ball and run with it.

SWEEP—A play where the ball carrier follows a group of teammates moving sideways to "sweep" the defense out of the way. A good sweep gives the runner a chance to gain a lot of yards before he is tackled or forced out of bounds.

Glossary

FOOTBALL WORDS TO KNOW

ALL-AROUND—Good at many different parts of the game.

ALL-PRO—An honor given to the best players at their position at the end of each season.

AMERICAN FOOTBALL CONFERENCE (AFC)—One of two groups of teams that make up the NFL. The winner of the AFC plays the winner of the NFC in the Super Bowl.

AMERICAN FOOTBALL LEAGUE (AFL)—The football league that began play in 1960 and later merged with the NFL.

BLOCKER—A player who protects the ball carrier with his body.

CANADIAN FOOTBALL LEAGUE (CFL)—A professional league in Canada that began play in 1958.

DRAFTED—Chosen from a group of the best college players. The NFL draft is held each spring.

EXPANSION DRAFT—A meeting where a new team to a league gets to choose players from other teams in the league.

EXPANSION TEAM—A team added to a league when it expands.

FREE AGENTS—Players who are allowed to sign with any team that wants them.

FUMBLE—A ball that is dropped by the player carrying it.

INTERCEPTED—Caught in the air by a defensive player.

NATIONAL FOOTBALL CONFERENCE (NFC)—One of two groups of teams that make up the NFL. The winner of the NFC plays the winner of the AFC in the Super Bowl.

NATIONAL FOOTBALL LEAGUE (NFL)—The league that started in 1920 and is still operating today.

PLAYOFFS—The games played after the season to determine which teams play in the Super Bowl.

PRO BOWL—The NFL's all-star game, played after the Super Bowl.

PROFESSIONAL—A player or team that plays a sport for money.

ROOKIES—Players in their first season.

ROOKIE OF THE YEAR—The annual award given to the league's best first-year player.

SACKED—Tackled the quarterback behind the line of scrimmage.

SOUTH DIVISION—A division for teams that play in the southern part of the country.

SUPER BOWL—The championship of football, played between the winners of the NFC and AFC.

TURNOVERS—Fumbles or interceptions that give possession of the ball to the opposing team.

VETERANS—Players with great experience.

WORLD FOOTBALL LEAGUE (WFL)—The league that tried to challenge the NFL in the 1970s. The WFL started in 1974 and ended in 1975.

OTHER WORDS TO KNOW

COMEBACK—The process of catching up from behind, or making up a large deficit.

DECADES—Periods of 10 years; also specific periods, such as the 1950s.

DISCOURAGED—Sad and disappointed.

EMERGE—Come into view.

INVESTORS—People who spend their money for the purpose of making more money.

LOGO—A symbol or design that represents a company or team.

MASCOT—An animal or person believed to bring a group good luck.

OVERPOWER—Control with strength and force.

RESEMBLE—Look like.

RETRACTABLE—Able to pull back.

RIVALRY—Extremely emotional competition.

STRATEGIES—Plans or methods for succeeding.

TAILBONE—The bone that protects the base of the spine.

TRADITION—A belief or custom that is handed down from generation to generation.

TRIBUTE—A way of showing respect.

Places to Go

ON THE ROAD

HOUSTON TEXANS
One Reliant Park
Houston, Texas 77054
(832) 667-2000

THE PRO FOOTBALL HALL OF FAME
2121 George Halas Drive NW
Canton, Ohio 44708
(330) 456-8207

ON THE WEB

THE NATIONAL FOOTBALL LEAGUE   www.nfl.com
  * *Learn more about the National Football League*

THE HOUSTON TEXANS   www.houstontexans.com
  * *Learn more about the Texans*

THE PRO FOOTBALL HALL OF FAME   www.profootballhof.com
  * *Learn more about football's greatest players*

ON THE BOOKSHELF

To learn more about the sport of football, look for these books at your library or bookstore:

  * Fleder, Rob–Editor. *The Football Book*. New York, New York: Sports Illustrated Books, 2005.

  * Kennedy, Mike. *Football*. Danbury, Connecticut: Franklin Watts, 2003.

  * Savage, Jeff. *Play by Play Football*. Minneapolis, Minnesota: Lerner Sports, 2004.

Index

PAGE NUMBERS IN **BOLD** REFER TO ILLUSTRATIONS.

Astrodome 13, 33

Boselli, Tony 7

Bradford, Corey 18

Brown, Kris 18, 28, **28**, 30, 43

Capers, Dom 7, 25,
31, 38, **38**, 43

Carr, David 9, **9**, **16**,
17, 18, 20, **20**,
26, **26**, 27, 31, 43

Carter, Quincy 18

Davis, Andre 27

Dayne, Ron **35**, 43

Dressen, Joel 39

Elway, John 25

Gaffney, Jabar **34**

Glenn, Aaron 7, **14**, 18,
19, 30, 31, 34

Johnson, Andre **4**, **8**, 9,
21, **21**, **32**, 35,
35, 36, 37, **37**, 43

Kubiak, Gary 11, 25, **25**, 38

Maddox, Tommy 30

Manning, Peyton 22

Mathis, Jerome 35, **35**, 36

McLane, Drayton 29

McNair, Bob 6, **6**, 29

McNair, Steve 26, 27

Miller, Billy 17, **17**

Okoye, Amobi **10**, 11, 23,
23, 37, 39, 43

Payne, Seth 18

Peek, Antwan 27

Reliant Stadium **12**, 16, 34

Rice, Jerry 37

Robinson, Dunta 11, 22,
22, 43, **43**

Ryans, DeMeco 11, **15**, 23,
23, 35, **35**,
38, 40, **41**, 43

Schaub, Matt **4**, **25**, 39, **39**

Sharper, Jamie 7, **7**, 21, 43

Simmons, James **31**

Tagliabue, Paul 16

Walker, Gary 7, 34, **34**

Williams, Domanick
  (also known as
  Domanick Davis) 9, 21, **21**,
36, **36**, 40, **40**, 43

Williams, Mario **10**, 11,
22, **22**, 29,
29, 39, 40, 43

Wong, Kailee 27

Wright, Kenny 30

Young, Vince 22, 29

The Team

MARK STEWART has written more than 20 books on football, and over 100 sports books for kids. He grew up in New York City during the 1960s rooting for the Giants and Jets, and now takes his two daughters, Mariah and Rachel, to watch them play in their home state of New Jersey. Mark comes from a family of writers. His grandfather was Sunday Editor of *The New York Times* and his mother was Articles Editor of *The Ladies' Home Journal* and *McCall's*. Mark has profiled hundreds of athletes over the last 20 years. He has also written several books about New York and New Jersey. Mark is a graduate of Duke University, with a degree in History. He lives with his daughters and wife Sarah overlooking Sandy Hook, New Jersey.

JASON AIKENS is the Collections Curator at the Pro Football Hall of Fame. He is responsible for the preservation of the Pro Football Hall of Fame's collection of artifacts and memorabilia and obtaining new donations of memorabilia from current players and NFL teams. Jason has a Bachelor of Arts in History from Michigan State University and a Master's in History from Western Michigan University where he concentrated on sports history. Jason has been working for the Pro Football Hall of Fame since 1997; before that he was an intern at the College Football Hall of Fame. Jason's family has roots in California and has been following the St. Louis Rams since their days in Los Angeles, California. He lives with his wife Cynthia and their daughter Angelina in Canton, Ohio.